Down by the River

Afro-Caribbean Rhymes, Games, and Songs for Children

Compiled by *Grace Hallworth*

Illustrated by *Caroline Binch*

Cartwheel
B·O·O·K·S®

SCHOLASTIC INC.
New York Toronto London Auckland Sydney

To Harold Rosen, who started all this,
to Ann Gift, Tobago librarian, who aided and abetted,
and to all those who shared childhood memories
G.H.

For Deborah and Tobago's children
C.B.

Text copyright © 1996 by Grace Hallworth.
Illustrations copyright © 1996 by Caroline Binch.
First American edition 1996. Originally published in Great Britain in 1996 by William Heinermann Ltd., an imprint
of Reed International Books, Michelin House, 81 Fulham Road, London SW3 6RB, and Auckland, Melbourne,
Singapore and Toronto. All rights reserved. Published by Scholastic Inc., 555 Broadway, New York, NY 10012 by
arrangement with Reed International Books.

CARTWHEEL BOOKS and the CARTWHEEL BOOKS logo are registered trademarks of Scholastic Inc.

Library of Congress Cataloging-in-Publication Data
Down by the river: Afro-Caribbean rhymes, games, and songs for children / [compiled] by Grace Hallworth;
illustrated by Caroline Binch. — 1st American ed.
     p.   cm.
Summary: Rhymes, chants, and games of Afro-Caribbean origin.
ISBN 0-590-69320-4 (alk. paper)
   1. Children's poetry, Caribbean (English)   2. Children's songs—Caribbean Area—Texts.   3. Caribbean
Area—Juvenile poetry.   4. Nursery rhymes.   [1. Caribbean literature (English)]
I. Hallworth, Grace.   II. Binch, Caroline, ill.
PR9205.6.D69   1996
811—dc20   96-2043
                                                                                                 CIP
                                                                                                  AC

12 11 10 9 8 7 6 5 4 3 2 1   6 7 8 9/9 0 1/0

Printed in China

First Scholastic printing, October 1996

INTRODUCTION

Most of the rhymes, songs, chants, and lullabies that you will find in this book are ones that I remember from my childhood. Others have been contributed by friends from Trinidad or from other islands in the Caribbean.

I grew up in Trinidad and I remember my childhood as quite carefree. I had three brothers and two sisters. Before I was eleven years old I had two places to call home. During the school term I lived with my aunt who was a school teacher, but at holiday times I lived at my parents' home.

My aunt's house was near the sea — it was just eight streets away. There were children in most of the houses in the neighborhood, so I had lots of friends.

Life at my aunt's house was ordered. There was music and adult conversation. I felt like an only child. Then, during the holidays, I was back in the noisy bustle of my larger family. At my parents' house, boys' games predominated. My brothers taught me how to spin tops, pitch marbles, and whistle.

In high school, I had the opportunity to meet children from many different backgrounds. We were a fantastic mix — Chinese, African, Asian, Portuguese, Spanish, English, Dutch, Jewish, French Creole, Syrian, and others. Although we represented so many races, our culture was the same — Trinidadian.

At the time, all these playground rhymes seemed ours alone. However, when I began to research them, I found that many of the singing and dancing games are European in origin, and that often the rhymes show traces of their French, African, English, and American roots.

For me, this is important. As children sing and play and then pass on the songs and games of their childhood, we see a living example of the inter-relationship of different cultures. This is something for us all to appreciate and respect.

GRACE HALLWORTH

WAKE-UP TIME

Pinchy, pinchy, pinchy,
Fly, fly away.

Birdy, birdy, birdy,
Fly, fly away.

Clap hands for Mama,
Till Daddy come;
Daddy bring cake an' sugar plum
An' give baby some.

PLAYTIME

Down by the river,
Down by the sea,
Johnny break a bottle
An' he say is me.
I tell Ma.
Ma tell Pa.
Johnny get a licking,
An' a ha! ha! ha!

One potato, two potato,
Three potato, four,
Five potato, six potato,
Seven potato,
More.

RAINY DAY RHYMES

Rain, rain,
Go to Spain,
And never come back
To Trinidad again.

Rain, rain,
Go away;
Come again
Another day.

*June is the start of the rainy season and
the beginning of hurricane weather.*

June too soon,
July stand by,
August come it must,
September remember,
October all over.

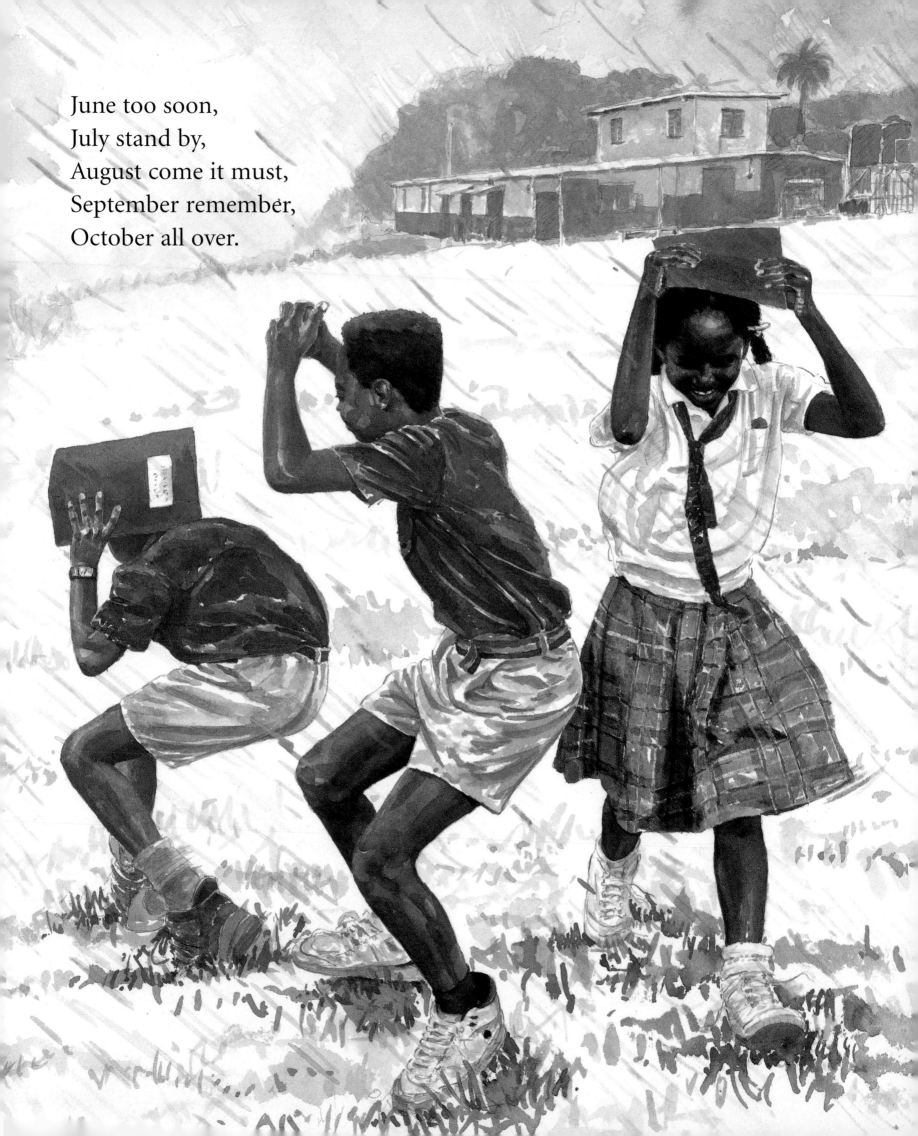

IN THE PLAYGROUND

One, two, three, four, five, six, seven,
All good children go to heaven.
The clock in heaven strikes eleven,
One, two, three, four, five, six, seven.

Out goes the lady with the seesaw hat;
O-U-T spells OUT,
And out goes you.

Ziggedy ziggedy marble stone,
Pointer pointer buff,
Buff ca-lay-lay,
Fee fee lay-lay,
Bim, bam, fire!

Ring-a-ding-ding,
The school bell ring.
Teacher knickers
Tie up with string.
String pop,
Knickers drop,
Teacher run out the room
Crying.

JUMPING ROPE

Bupsi-ky-sico pindar shell.
Miss say bupsi-ky-sico pindar shell.
I love coffee. I love tea.
I love the girls and the girls love me.

Miss Sue, Miss Sue,
From out of Ballou,
She's having a party,
Chika boom,
Chicka boom-boom-boom.
Let's do the tip-tap-toe.
Mama's got the cold;
Papa's got the flu.
I ain't lying,
And neither are you.
Sitting in the palace
Peeling white potatoes;
Sitting in the alley
Drinking Black Labels.
Listen to the clock go,
Chit-chit chi wa-wa,
Chit-chit chi wa-wa,
FREEZE!

CLAP HANDS

Mosquito one,
Mosquito two,
Mosquito jump in de callaloo.

Mosquito three,
Mosquito four,
Mosquito fly out de ol' man door.

Mosquito five,
Mosquito six,
Mosquito break up de ol' man bricks.

Mosquito seven,
Mosquito eight,
Mosquito open de ol' man gate.

Mosquito nine,
Mosquito ten,
Mosquito tickle de ol' man hen.

Callaloo is a spinach dish.

CHOOSE YOUR PARTNER

This way, Valerie,
That way, Valerie,
This way, Valerie,
All day long.

Here comes the pretty one,
Just like the other one;
Here comes the pretty one,
All day long.

This way, Valerie,
That way, Valerie,
This way, Valerie,
All day long.

BROWN GIRL IN THE RING

This is a circle game with one child in the middle performing the actions.

There's a brown girl in the ring,
Tra la-la-la-la.
There's a brown girl in the ring,
Tra la-la-la-la.
A brown girl in the ring,
Tra la-la-la-la,
For she's sweet like a sugar
And a plum, plum, plum.

Now show me your motion,
Tra la-la-la-la.
Now show me your motion,
Tra la-la-la-la.
Now show me your motion,
Tra la-la-la-la,
For she's sweet like a sugar
And a plum, plum, plum.

Now hug and kiss your partner,
Tra la-la-la-la.
Now hug and kiss your partner,
Tra la-la-la-la.
Now hug and kiss your partner,
Tra la-la-la-la,
For she's sweet like a sugar
And a plum, plum, plum.

GOING SHOPPING

One day, one day,
Congotay.

I went down the bay,
Congotay.

I meet an ol' lady,
Congotay.

With a box of chickens,
Congotay.

I ask her for one,
Congotay.

But she wouldn't give me,
Congotay.

She's a greedy Mama,
Congotay.

So I took it anyway,
Congotay.

"Congotay" is an alternating chant game in which two lines of children stand facing each other with the leader (Mama) of one side protecting the children (chickens) behind her.

I diggin' potatoes,
John belly gros.

All roun' de harbor,
John belly gros.

An' coo coo in de fire,
John belly gros.

An' de cat can't catch me,
John belly gros.

Coo coo is a dish of cornmeal and okra cooked in butter.

FRIENDSHIPS

Blue, blue,
Your love is true.
Red, red,
You wet your bed.
Green, green,
You eat ice cream.
Pink, pink,
You smelling stink.
Yellow, yellow,
You kiss a fellow.
White, white,
You fly a kite.
Brown, brown,
You go to town
In your dirty washekong.
Black, black,
You break my back.

Washekong are sneakers.

TAUNTS AND TEASES

Tit for tat,
Butter for fat;
Yo' kill m' dog,
I go kill yo' cat.

Spider bring money.
Spider bring luck.
If yo' kill a spider,
All yo' life yo' will work.

Cry, cry baby,
Wallow, wallow, dumpling,
Push yo' finger in yo' eye,
An' tell yo' mother it was I.

WE DON'T CARE!

*As the "children" answer "Mama," they creep
closer and closer to her until finally "Mama"
turns and chases them.*

Children, children.
Yes, Mama.

Where yo' been to?
Granmama.

What she give yo'?
Two apples.

Where yo' put them?
On the shelf.

How will yo' get them?
Stand on a chair.

Suppose yo' fall?
We don't care.

I'll beat yo' tonight.
We'll tell Papa!

BACK HOME

Johnny was a maker,
Live in Jamaica.
Had three daughters,
Name Jamaica.
Jump through the window,
Broke m' little finger.
Timba, timba,
Inganglo.
Bend down low,
Inganglo.
Me Mama broke m' toe,
Inganglo.
Fela, fela,
Inganglo.

TIME FOR BED

Baby mine, oh, baby mine,
Now go to sleep;
Close your little sleepy eyes
And dream sweet dreams.

Dodo, petit po-po,
Mama coming just now;
Dodo, petit po-po,
Mama coming just now.

ENDINGS

Fall on de wire,
De wire bend;
And that's the way,
The story end.

Cric crac,
Monkey break he back,
For a rotten pomerac.

A pomerac is a fruit.